Ancient Rome

*A Concise Overview of the Roman History
and Mythology Including the Rise and Fall
of the Roman Empire*

Eric Brown

inattention, use, or misuse of the information in question by the reader will render any resulting actions solely under his purview. There are no scenarios in which the publisher or the original author of this work can be deemed liable for any hardship or damage that may befall the reader after undertaking any information described herein.

Additionally, the contents of the following pages are intended only for informational purposes; thus, it should be thought of as universal. As befitting its nature, it is presented without assurance regarding its prolonged validity or interim quality. Trademarks that are mentioned are done without written consent and can in no way be considered an endorsement from the trademark holder.

Table of Contents

Introduction

Congratulations on downloading *Ancient Rome* and thank you for doing so.

Few societies and historical periods capture our fascination as much as ancient Rome. With a founding steeped in legend, along with the rise and fall of a monarchy, a republic, and an empire filled with colorful, and often even bizarre, leaders and popular figures, it is no wonder that it has been the source of inspiration for a multitude of novels, movies, and television shows. While this entertainment fare has had varying degrees of historical accuracy, a great deal of artistic license does not need to be taken to make the story of ancient Rome intriguing and scintillating. It was a society and a people rich with drama that still captures our interest even today, more than 1500 years since the fall of the great Roman Empire.

There are many books on this subject on the market; nonetheless, thank you once again for choosing this one! Every effort was made to fill it with as much useful information as possible. Please enjoy!

Chapter 1: The Founding of Rome and Rise of a Republic

Remus and Romulus

The story of the founding of Rome is one steeped in legend and enough drama to rival any modern-day soap opera or novella. The mythology of its origin centers on the twin brothers, Romulus and Remus, who were known in various legends to be the sons of a mortal woman and either the god, Mars, or the demigod, Hercules. The woman, Rhea Silvia, was the daughter of Numitor, the deposed king of Alba Longa, a city in the central area of the Italian peninsula. Rhea Silva was forced to take vows of chastity as a Vestal Virgin, a priestess in service to the goddess of home and hearth, Vesta. This was to prevent her from producing heirs who might renew claims to the throne.

Fearing that the divinely conceived twins might become rivals for his title, the usurper king of Alba Longa, Amulius, who was also Rhea Silvia's uncle, ordered that the twin infants be killed. He stipulated that their murders should be through drowning, a method chosen to prevent possible retribution from the gods. Taking even further care to avoid having the blood of his kin on his hands, Amulius relegated the murderous task to a servant, who was instructed to cast the boys into the River Tiber. The

8

servant was unable to carry out the task, however, taking pity on the infants. Instead, he sent them down the river in a basket.

Legend holds that the river god, Tiberinus, calmed the waters to ensure the twin's safe journey, and assisted in letting the basket reach the riverbank at the base of one of the Seven Hills of Rome, the Palatine. After washing ashore, they were found by a she-wolf, or Lupa, that suckled them. The animal kept them alive until they were discovered and taken in by a shepherd named Faustulus and his wife, Acca Larentia. The boys were raised by Faustulus as his own sons. They grew up to become shepherds, following in the footsteps of the man who adopted them.

There are several variations of the story on how the twins eventually discovered their true identities and confrontation that followed with Amulius, their great uncle and the still-sitting king who had ordered their deaths. Yet, all versions of the legend agree that Remus and Romulus killed Amulius. They then declined the offer to take the throne of Alba Longa, preferring instead to establish a new city and return the title back to their grandfather, Numitor.

Upon determining to found a new city of their own, the brothers argued about the appropriate location. Romulus believed that it should be at the site where they had washed ashore as infants, near the Palatine. Remus was of another mind, however, choosing to settle near another part of the Seven Hills, the Aventine. Unable to come to an agreement, they determined to leave the decision to the hands of the gods by seeking signs of prophecy in the natural world, a practice termed as augury.

Unfortunately, this also failed to settle the conflict, since they disagreed on the meaning and significance of the signs that they had seen. Refusing to remain at an impasse, Romulus decided to move forward with the construction of a new city at the Palatine even without his twin's assent. This further deepened the conflict between them. What began as a petty quarrel tragically ended in fratricide. Romulus killed his brother and crowned himself king of the new settlement. He called it *Roma,* or what we now know as "Rome," after his own name.

The Roman Monarchy (753 – 509 BCE)

Romulus' taking of the throne as the first king of the new city, which is understood as having been in 753 BCE, is acknowledged as the beginning of the Roman Monarchy. This was a period of nearly 250 years that was marked by the development of a new system of government, a number of unusual measures that were intended to increase the population of the city, and a series of conflicts and wars with neighboring cities and peoples.

The Senate

One of Romulus' innovations in government was the establishment of a 100-member Senate, or *senatus*. The literal meaning of the word, which was that of a "gathering of old men," indicates both its constitution and practical function in the monarchy. Consisting of individuals from the upper ranks of society and those with a great deal of experience in public service, the Senate primarily served in an advisory capacity to the city's elected officials called the magistrates. While the Senate was not empowered with law-making capacities, its guidance and decisions were highly influential in the adoption of new laws.

As a position in the Senate was a highly influential one, those who held the rank were entitled to certain practical and social privileges. These ranged from special financial opportunities and benefits to preferred seating at public events and the wearing of distinguished garments and accessories. A specific hue known as Tyrian purple was associated with royalty and the highest positions of honor in ancient Rome. It was a color that was difficult to produce for use in fabrics, with the extraction of its pigment requiring the use of thousands of a certain type of marine snail. The scarcity of the components and the complexity of the process of producing the color made it as one that denoted a high social rank. Senators were permitted to wear a strip of purple on their togas, and wore rings signifying their membership in the important government body.

The Senate could gather anywhere within the city or its immediate outskirts as long as the meeting place was deemed sacred such as a temple, or *templum*. They gathered most often in a public building known as the Curia. Its precise structure, however, changed over the years through the different periods of the monarchy, Republic, and Imperial Rome. The Curia was open to the public, as were the meetings. Anyone was allowed to attend, and people often did sit outside of the Curia to listen in on important and influential debates and discussions among the senators.

Yet even with the existence of a senate, most of the power and authority in the Roman monarchy rested in the hands of the king. The king had full control over law-making, political measures and policies, the appointment of public officials, and military activities and issues. He even had the final word in religious matters. Any dispute could be decided by the king, who was recognized as the final and ultimate authority.

Population Development

When Romulus founded Rome, he encouraged population growth by inviting and welcoming everyone who wished to become a resident of the city, no matter what sort of past that individual might have. Consequently, large numbers of people with criminal histories were attracted to Rome, as were former slaves and freemen, most of whom were male.

This open-door approach was extremely effective in boosting citizenship, and the population of Rome rapidly increased. This led to the necessity of expanding the city beyond its original site of the Palatine, to encompass three more of the other Seven Hills. One of these was Aventine, Remus' choice for the initial settlement.

The policy resulted in a population that was overwhelmingly male, which was not conducive to either a satisfied citizenry or to long-term population growth. In historical accounts of early Rome, it is said that Romulus initially tried to deal with this issue by negotiating with neighboring towns, cities, and societies, to encourage female members of their populations to marry Roman men.

When those negotiations proved unsuccessful, Romulus conceived a scheme to kidnap a large number of women from the Sabines, a group of people living in the central area of the Apennine Mountains. To achieve this desired end, Romulus planned an elaborate festival to honor the god, Neptune, and invited the residents of the surrounding areas to attend. It is said that at some point in the festival, the Sabine women were abducted while their male counterparts were attacked, killed, or driven off.

This event was known as "The Rape of the Sabine Women." The terminology has been subject to much debate, both historically and at the present day, with many holding that it was characterized by kidnapping and abduction, not assault. Yet one of the grounds upon which the Sabine women were enticed or coerced into marrying Roman men is recorded as having involved a plea for the "common children." The plea, purportedly delivered to all Sabine women individually by Romulus himself, suggested that many may have been impregnated during the time of their abduction.

Whatever the actual details may have been, the effort served to instigate the first of Rome's wars, fought against the Sabines, and from which Rome emerged victorious. After being defeated, the Sabines entered into a treaty with Rome, agreeing to the merging of their populations and to a joint rulership of the resultant society. This cooperative endeavor gave rise to a merging of cultures, with both peoples adopting each other's customs and practices. This is something that would come to characterize ancient Roman society throughout the full span of its existence.

As the population grew, Romulus divided his citizens into tribes based on their areas of origin and ethnicity. The Sabines represented one tribe, as did the Etruscans, with the third tribe being the Roman people. The post-treaty joint rulership with the Sabines brought five years of peace and relative harmony until the Sabine king, Tatius, sheltered and then freed criminal fugitives, leading to his assassination. Thus, Romulus was left as the sole king with full authority over the new, merged society.

The Passing of Romulus

For the following two decades, Rome continued to expand, increasing its territory and populace through war and, when Romulus' grandfather died, through inheritance. As Rome grew, so did the king's handle on power. While there is very little historical information that accurately recounts the factual events, it is commonly believed that Romulus' increasingly autocratic methods sparked resentment in the Senate, who begrudged the loss of their influence on public matters.

Some sources suggest that Romulus was ultimately assassinated by the Senate or by those operating under its instructions. Others assert that his demise was as divinely influenced as his conception, claiming that eyewitnesses have attested to the fact that he mysteriously disappeared during a storm that had interrupted a religious ceremony in 717 BCE. In some accounts, it is reported that he became a god upon his death. Such a report has contributed to speculation that the story of Romulus and his brother, Remus, was a myth, and not the history of actual men.

The Line of Kings

The Roman monarchy continued after Romulus' reign and death. Whether it was real or fable, his succession saw a series of kings with varying personalities and goals, each contributing to the growth and evolution of the city and culture of Rome.

A brief overview of the kings and some of their notable features and contributions:

Numa Pompilius

Years of rule: 715 - 673 BCE

Numa was a member of the Sabine tribe who was more interested in living a solitary life, studying religion and philosophy, than ruling. He reluctantly accepted the title of king; doing so only after consulting an augury to determine the wishes of the gods regarding his fate.

Known for:

- Adding January and February to the annual calendar, increasing the number of days in a year to 360.

- Relocating the order of priestesses of Vesta, the Vestal Virgins, from Alba Longa to Rome.

- Marking the borders of the Roman territory.

- Allotting land to farmers of the peasant class to ensure

consistent food production and supply.

- Establishing an order of priests, the Fetiale collegium, to serve as ambassadors and advise the Senate on international treaties and measures of war and peace.

- Creating a role of a head priest to oversee all religious activities, called a *Pontifex Maximus*.

- Introducing professional guilds to Rome to alleviate tensions between the tribal groups.

Numa is recognized as having been a peaceful and thoughtful leader who initiated many institutions and practices that continued to live on long after his period of rule.

Tullus Hostilius

Years of rule: 673 - 641 BCE

Unlike his predecessor who was known as a man of peace, Tullus is characterized as a war hawk. He had little regard for the wishes of the gods; shunning religious ceremonies until a string of events transpired that caused him to become increasingly superstitious. Yet, like the first king of the monarchy, Romulus, many scholars question his existence as a real historical figure due to a number of inconsistencies in the work attributed to him.

Known for:

- Being warlike and consistently engaging in campaigns throughout his rule.

- Improving the organization of the Roman army.

- Incorporating Alba Longa into Rome.

- Establishing the *Curia Hostilia*, the first formal chamber for Senate meetings, which included an exterior area for citizens to meet and vote on public matters, the *Comitium*.

Along with other similarities to Romulus, it is said that Hostilius also died during a storm, allegedly struck down by a lightning bolt sent by the god, Jupiter.

Ancus Marcius

Years of rule: 641 -616 BCE

Grandson of the second king of Rome, Marcius is noted for having borne a number of similarities with Numa, including a peaceful agenda and a desire to improve matters related to Rome's cultural and social affairs.

Known for:

- Expanding Rome to encompass another of the Seven Hills, the Janiculum, to accommodate an ever-growing population, and for its strategic location.

- Establishing the coastal port of Ostia, improving access

to trade with other cities, towns, and peoples of the Mediterranean.

Due to his likeness to Numa, Marcius was initially mistaken for being a weak king and consequently faced challenges that resulted in war. He ultimately proved himself to be a strong and capable military leader.

Lucius Tarquinius Priscus (Tarquin the Elder)

Years of rule: 616 - 579 BCE

Tarquin rose through the ranks of Roman political society and became a close ally of Marcius; even being named as guardian of his sons. While the hereditary rule was not yet in place during the monarchy, Tarquin feared that the kingship will go to Marcius' heirs upon his death. He successfully plotted to acquire the throne.

Known for:

- His plot to secure the throne from Marcius' sons.

- Making many reforms to the Roman army, such as increasing the size of the cavalry.

- Introducing a number of Etruscan elements into the symbols and insignia associated with the Roman throne.

Tarquin's plotting against Marcius' sons for possession of the throne eventually caught up with him, as they ultimately hired assassins to kill him with the blow of an ax. His wife and his adopted son (some sources define him as a close friend), Servius Tullius, hid his death from the people. Servius then established himself as an interim ruler while Tarquin purportedly recovered from his wounds. When the truth about his death finally came to light, Servius had served long enough to be proven a competent leader, and his claim to the throne was unchallenged.

Servius Tullius

Years of rule: 579 - 535 BCE

Servius was believed by many in Rome to have been in line for a great destiny since the time of his infancy, when it was reported that a ring of fire appeared around his head, while the rest of his body remained unharmed. He aligned himself with Tarquin the Elder, which resulted in his ascension to the throne after the king's death. His claim was further strengthened by the marriage of his two daughters to Tarquin's two sons.

Known for:

- Having such a resounding triumph over Etruscan forces in battle, that he was able to avoid another war for the rest of his reign, which lasted 44 years.

- Introducing a census.

- Extending voting rights to certain classes of common, or lower, citizens.

- Creating tensions between the upper and lower classes, the Patricians and the Plebeians, by making decisions favorable to the latter.

The conflicts that arose from Servius' activities and actions that favored the lower classes, combined with the somewhat questionable way in which he had gained the throne, compelled his youngest daughter to conspire with Tarquin's son, Lucius Tarquinius. They arranged for his murder, which occurred on the steps of the Curia.

Lucius Tarquinius Superbus (Tarquin the Proud)

Years of rule: 534 - 509 BCE

After conspiring in the death of Servius, Lucius claimed the throne as the last of the kings of the monarchy. He earned the suffix of "Superbus," which translates to "arrogant," due to his personality and the ruthlessness of his actions in the murder of his predecessor.

Known for:

- Being a harsh, oppressive, and power-hungry ruler who utilized the tools of manipulation and intimidation in exercising his authority and control.

- Steadily working to diminish the rights and controls of

the upper classes and the Senate.

- Doubling Rome's military power by forcing neighboring towns and cities to cede control of their armies to his authority.

- Engaging in constant construction projects, sometimes destroying the sacred buildings of other tribes.

- Inspiring rebellion and the overthrow and abandonment of the monarchy.

The straw that broke the camel's back, as the saying goes, which inspired rebellion and the subsequent overthrow of Superbus in 509 BCE, was an act of rape. The despicable deed was done by his son to a Roman consul's wife, Lucretia. She shared an account of the experience with her husband and father before killing herself, distraught from shame. This stirred the public's anger and led to an uprising, which sent the king into exile and marked the end of the period of the monarchy.

The Roman Republic (509 – 27 BCE)

Outraged and no longer tolerant to the idea of a one-man rule by a monarch after the oppressive reign of Tarquin the Proud, the senate and people of Rome determined that a new king would not be elected. Instead, the Senate would exercise primary control of the state. The role of the king was divided into two positions serving as heads of state, annually elected magistrates called consuls.

It was thought that having two individuals in equal positions of power would help to prevent one or the other from over-reaching and attempting to exercise excessive control. To further prevent corruption and political decisions that could work against the best interest of Rome as a whole, the Senate determined that consuls would be held legally accountable for their actions. They can face prosecution, even after their annual term, for any misdeed committed during their year in power.

The era of the Republic was marked by a large expansion of territory, pushing Rome's borders further outward. This was facilitated by numerous victories in a long series of wars, which was another notable feature of this era.

There were struggles on the domestic front as well. A major one that the city and Senate contended with during the period of the Republic was the increasing conflict that resulted from deep class divisions within Roman society. The massive divide between the classes sparked a series of civil wars, each driven on both sides by powerful individuals who roused support from the people, to further causes in the effort to address disparities in status and opportunity among the Romans.

A String of Wars

The Roman Republic was engaged in a series of wars and conflicts, both internally and externally. It not only influenced the size and shape of its overall territory but also relationships within the populace and with outside peoples.

Samnite Wars (343 - 282 BCE)

Rome engaged in three wars fought over a 61-year period with the Samnite Kingdom, which was located on the east of Rome. Due to its location, it posed a threat of meaningful proportions to the territories of the Republic.

The First Samnite War is difficult to accurately chronicle because of the engagement of so many parties and the variety of shifting alliances. Even the historians of the day had a difficult time keeping track of specific events and their significance. However, it is generally understood that Rome became involved when it sought to assist people who were living in the nearby highlands, against attacks from the Samnites and other groups.

The Second Samnite War was a power struggle that lasted for 22 years, focused on the control over the city of Naples. It was a long conflict that resulted in heavy losses on both sides; however, Rome eventually dominated and asserted its hold over the central region of the Italian peninsula.

The Third Samnite War involved the collaboration of Gauls, Umbrians, Etruscans, and Samnites, in a bid to defeat Rome. Yet, the Republic was ultimately successful in spite of the impressive alliance formed by its enemies. After this victory, the Roman dominance of central Italy was assured and unchallenged.

Pyrrhic Wars – 280 to 275 BCE

The Pyrrhic wars were fought between Tarentum and Rome. Pyrrhic refers to the king of Epirus in Greece, Pyrrhus. The Tarentum was a Spartan colony located in the Southern Italian coast.

The war started when Roman warships sailed through the bay in Tarentum in order to protect Thurii. This violated a treaty with Tarentum, which forbade the Romans to sail past the Lacinian Promontory of Croton.

Tarentines were not hesitant at all, and they soon sank five of Rome's ten vessels. Rome quickly declared war. As a result, Tarentum contacted Pyrrhus for help.

There were three major battles in the Pyrrhic war:

- Battle of Heraclea in 280 BCE – Pyrrhic victory

- Battle of Asculum in 279 BCE – Pyrrhic victory

- Battle of Beneventum in 275 BCE – Roman victory

In the end, Rome won the war when they laid siege to the city of Tarentum in 272 BCE.

Punic Wars – 264 to 146 BCE

There were three Punic wars that took place between Rome and Carthage. They started in 264 BCE and ended when Carthage was destroyed in 146 BCE. Throughout the Italian peninsula, Rome had become a dominant power before the First Punic War broke out. Carthage, on the other hand, was a powerful city-state located in Northern Africa and was widely known for its maritime strength.

Rome, in 264 BCE, decided to intervene in a dispute between Sicily, a Carthaginian province at that time, and Messina, which involved an attack by Syracuse soldiers against Messina. Carthage sided with Syracuse while Rome sided with Messina. The disagreement eventually exploded in a war that pitted these two powers, with Sicily at stake. Within the 20 years that formed part of the lengthy conflict, Rome rebuilt its fleet so it could confront Carthage's navy. The Roman ships scored their first sea victory at Mylae in 260 BCE, although their invasion of North Africa was not so successful. By the end of the First Punic War, Rome took over the control of Sicily as its first overseas province.

Before the Second Punic War began, Rome had gained dominance over Sardinia and Corsica. Carthage, though, had managed to create an influence over Spain by 237 BCE, under the leadership of Hamilcar Barca and his then son-in-law, Hasdrubal. Legend says that Barca died in 229 BCE and made his younger son, Hannibal, swear a blood oath against Rome. When Hasdrubal died in 221 BCE, Hannibal took charge of the Carthaginian forces in Spain. In two years, he led his army into Saguntum, an Iberian city under Roman protection. Thus, the Second Punic War began.

Hannibal gained quite a few victories during his march from Spain to Italy. His conquest reached its height at Cannae in 216 BCE when his cavalry surrounded Rome's. Rome rebounded, and the Carthaginians soon lost their hold over Italy after Roman victories in North Africa and Spain. Hannibal's troops had to abandon their fight in Italy so they could defend North Africa. Hannibal's losses put an end to Carthage's empire in the Western Mediterranean. Spain became a territory of Rome and Carthage was left with only its North African territory.

The third war was the most controversial, started by Cato the Elder and other members of the Roman Senate who tried to convince their colleagues that Carthage was still a threat to Rome's supremacy. Technically speaking, Carthage did break their treaty with Rome in 149 BCE, when they declared war against Numidia. After the war began, the Carthaginians held their own for two years, until the Romans put Scipio Aemilianus in charge of their North African campaign. In 146

BCE, Aemilianus pushed his way into the citadel. After seven days of fighting, Carthage finally surrendered. The war obliterated the 700-year-old city, and its 50,000 surviving citizens were sold into slavery.

Servile Wars - 135 to 71 BCE

There were three slave revolts during this period. The first one took place in Sicily and was led by a slave named Eunus who believed that he had supernatural powers. Cleon was his general and they resisted the Roman forces that were sent to control them. They used guerrilla tactics instead of open warfare. It took Rome three years to kill Cleon and capture Eunus.

After 22 years, another revolt arose in Sicily. However, not much is known about this particular war. It took several years to end as well.

The third conflict forming part of the Servile Wars occurred right in the Italian mainland. An escaped Gladiator, Spartacus, led the slave forces. The Roman Senate did not take the revolt seriously until several militias were defeated. After Spartacus was able to fight off two teams of Roman soldiers, thousands of slaves joined him in the mountains, bringing their ranks up to 70,000. Spartacus met his first defeat in Cisalpine Gaul in 72 BCE, where 20,000 of his men were killed. Still, newcomers continued to join him. Nobody really knows what motivated

Spartacus to do so; but, instead of escaping over the Alps, he went back to Southern Italy. In the final battle, Rome had upped its forces and Spartacus knew there was no way out. He and many of his soldiers were killed in the last campaign.

The Decline of the Roman Republic

At this point in the Roman Republic, things started to take a darker turn. The government was not working effectively and there was much civil unrest.

Tribune of the Plebeians

After the Roman Republic was established, the Plebeians were burdened with debts. This caused a series of clashes and almost brought the Plebeians to the brink of revolt. Instead, Lucius Sicinius Vellutus convinced them into seceding. The Senate sent in Agrippa Menenius Lanatus to talk to the group. They worked together and created the first tribune of Plebeians.

They became the most important check on the power of the magistrates and Roman Senate. They could preside over the people's assembly, intervene on behalf of the Plebeians in legal issues, propose legislation, and summon the Senate. Their biggest power was the capability to veto the actions of consuls.

Tiberius Gracchus – 133 BCE

Tiberius was a Roman tribune who died in 133 BCE. He sponsored agrarian reforms in order to restore the class of independent farmers. He was assassinated during a riot that was sparked by his opponents in the Senate.

He was born to an aristocratic Roman family. His education in the New Greek enlightenment gave him form and clarity in public speaking. Serving in the Roman military, he came to know about the weakness of Rome. This is what led him to secure a spot on the tribune.

Gaius Gracchus – 122 BCE

Gaius, the brother of Tiberius, was a Roman tribune from 123 to 122 BCE. He worked to reenact the agrarian reform that Tiberius had proposed. After his brother's murder, he joined the outcry against the Scipio Nasica.

While a complete understanding of his tribune career is uncertain because of some ambiguities in chronology, it is clear that he completed his program.

Pompey and Crassus

After Sulla removed the tribune, Pompey and Crassus, in 70 BCE, stood for consul election even though neither of them was legally allowed to do so. Crassus had to wait a year between his praetorship and consulship, and Pompey was too young. Nevertheless, they both ended up winning. They annulled the changes that Sulla made and restored power to the tribune. The Senate did not try to prevent them from doing this because both men had the support of loyal armies.

Julius Caesar

When Caesar took charge, he changed the course of history for the Greco-Roman world in a decisive and irreversible way. The Caesars family belonged to the patrician class, but this did not assure political advantage anymore. On the contrary, it was a handicap because family members were debarred from holding para-constitutional offices. The Caesars were not the snobbish or conservative-minded type of Patricians.

Caesar was born on July 12, 100 BCE. He carried his father's name. Caesar's father governed the province of Asia as praetor. Caesar's mother was Aurelia Cotta, who was also of noble birth. He was raised by parents who held a Populare ideology of Rome. This view favored a democratization of the government and wanted the Plebeians to be given better rights, as opposed to the views of the Optimate faction.

It is important to note that the Populare and the Optimate were not political parties in conflict like the ones we have today. Instead, they were political ideologies which a lot of people shifted towards and from, no matter what their class was in society. The concept of appealing to people who supported him, rather than trying to gain the approval of the members of the Senate or of the other Patricians, would end up helping Caesar later on.

Caesar's father died when he was 16, and he became the head of the family. He believed that being part of the priesthood would help his family the most. He was able to get himself nominated a High Priest of Jupiter. In order to qualify for the position, one had to be a patrician and be married to another  patrician. Because of these rules, Caesar had to break off his engagement with a plebeian girl.

In 84 BCE, Caesar married a patrician by the name of Cornelia, the daughter of Lucius Cornelius Cinna. The marriage publicly placed him on the radical side. Once Sulla declared himself as a dictator, he started a purge of his enemies, especially those who held the Populare ideology. Sulla ordered Caesar to divorce his wife but he refused. His defiance caused Caesar to be targeted, and he fled from Rome. His title was stripped and his wife's dowry was taken away.

Caesar left Italy and joined the military service in order to support his family. He proved to be a good soldier and was awarded the civic crown when he saved a life during battle.

After Sulla's death, Caesar returned to Rome and tried his hand at being an orator. He turned out to be an eloquent speaker.

While sailing to Greece in 75 BCE, a group of pirates kidnapped Caesar and held him for ransom. He always had a high opinion of himself, and when he was told that he was being held for 20 talents, Caesar said that he was worth at least fifty. During his captivity, the pirates treated him well and he made sure to stay friendly with them. He repeatedly told the pirates that once he was released, he would find and then crucify them for hurting his family. They thought that he was only joking. However, when he was released, he made good on this threat. He found the pirates and had their throats slit before being crucified.

Working with Pompey, Caesar worked to undo the Sullan constitution. In 65 BCE, Caesar was elected one of the curule aediles. During this time, he lived lavishly on borrowed money. In 63 BCE, he became pontifex maximus through a political dodge. At this point, he had established himself as a controversial political figure.

First Triumvirate

The First Triumvirate was established with the alliance of Crassus, Pompey, and Julius Caesar. The trio dominated the Roman Republic from 60 BCD to 53 BCE. The unstable government and a near civil war caused these three men to set aside their opposing views and join forces, controlling the

Roman political world for almost a decade. Julius Caesar eventually rose above all the other two.

The three knew that, together, they could achieve their goals. Caesar first had to reconcile the differences between Crassus and Pompey. In order to seal their alliance, Caesar had his daughter, Julie, marry Pompey.

Once Caesar's consulship ended, he moved his army over the Alps and into Gaul. He returned to Italy in 50 BCE, victorious. Pompey, however, was jealous of his success. He eventually became governor of Spain. Crassus was awarded an army but never realized his goals because he was killed in the Battle of Carrhae in 53 BCE. His death spelled doom for the triumvirate. The death of Caesar's daughter, Julia, split the alliance even further.

Pompey eventually fled to Egypt where the Egyptians had him murdered because they believed the gods favored Caesar. Caesar took off to Egypt to pursue Pompey, and was outraged when he found out that he had been killed. He proclaimed martial law and took over.

Caesar, in secret, sent for Cleopatra VII. She had been exiled and had herself smuggled through enemy lines. He aligned himself with her, starting a war between the Egyptian army and Caesar's legions. They were besieged in the palace by the Egyptians before Roman reinforcements showed up six months later, on March of 47 BCE. They then defeated the Egyptian army.

Cleopatra and Caesar had become lovers during this short meeting, and he stayed with her in Egypt for nine months. In 47 BCE, Cleopatra gave birth to a son, Ptolemy Caesar, who was most commonly known as Caesarion. The boy was named as her successor and heir.

During this time, Pharnaces created a rebellion in the East and Caesar left to crush it, leaving Cleopatra as Egypt's ruler. Caesar's troops marched through Asia Minor and defeated the tribes. He then turned his focus back to the people in Rome. During the Battle of Thapsus, Caesar's troops were able to defeat the forces of the Optimate faction. He returned to Rome, triumphant, in July of 46 BCE.

Cleopatra had hoped that Caesar would legitimize Caesarion as his son and heir. He didn't. Instead, he chose to name Gaius Octavius Thurinus, his grandnephew, as his heir. He did allow Cleopatra and their son, as well as their entourage, to move to a comfortable home in Rome. He visited them frequently even though he was already married to Calpurnia. The Senate was very upset with this, as Rome had strict laws against bigamy. Still, Caesar was designated as Dictator Perpetuus, giving him the title of dictator for life.

He initiated several reforms that included land redistribution for the veterans and the poor, which would eliminate the need for displacement of other citizens. He also devised political reforms that ended up being unpopular with the Senate. He did not rule with the Senate's approval in mind. He typically told them the laws that he wanted to have passed, and how quickly they should be done. All of these were done in the hopes of advancing and consolidating his power.

He changed the calendar, created a police force, and had the Carthage rebuilt. He also got rid of the tax system, among several other pieces of legislation. During the time that he ruled as a dictator, Romans enjoyed prosperous times. However, members of the Senate, especially those leaning towards the Optimate faction, were worried that he would end up becoming too powerful. They feared that he might get rid of the Senate altogether.

In 44 BCE, on March 15th, while at the portico of the basilica of Pompey the Great, Caesar was assassinated by a group of senators. One of the most well-known assassins was Marcus Junius Brutus, Caesar's second choice for his heir. Gaius Cassius Longinus was also an assassin. There were other assassins as well. Some stories say that there may have been as many as sixty.

Caesar ended up being stabbed 23 times before he died on the base of the statue of Pompey. The problem for the assassins was that they never made a plan on what to do after they killed

Caesar. By neglecting this part of their mission, they did not get rid of Marcus Antonius, Caesar's cousin, and right-hand man. Mark Antony turned the tables on the killers, partnering with Octavian and using Rome's popular opinion against the perpetrators.

Second Triumvirate

After the murder of Julius Caesar in 44 BCE, Octavian, Mark Antony, and Lepidus formed the Second Triumvirate. The three men vowed that they would get revenge on the killers and would stabilize the Roman Republic, in what ended up being its death throes.

The assassins of Caesar had believed that by killing him, they would bring back the faith and spirit that the Roman people used to have in the Republic. Without an exit strategy, Brutus fled to the Theater of Pompey. The Senate had gathered at the Temple of Jupiter on Capitoline Hill to address the citizens. They had expected a warm reception but this was not the case. The people were hostile towards them and did not like the Senate's pleas for amnesty and compromise. The assassins had to flee the city, with Cassius and Brutus making their way to the East.

The new triumvirate was, at best, unstable. Mark Antony and Octavian distrusted each other. Each of them believed that he was the rightful heir to lead the government. Antony added fuel to the fire when he blocked Octavian from gaining access to his stepfather's money. Lepidus, who was the most ineffective of the three, was named the Chief Priest. Antony appointed him even though the title was supposed to have been given to Octavian.

Antony was viewed by the Senate as an even more dangerous tyrant. He tried to take control over the government after Caesar's death and brought about the ire of the Senate. All of this ended up causing its members to declare Antony an enemy. Eventually, Lepidus was also declared an enemy after he voiced out his support of Antony. Antony managed to anger a number of important Roman citizens. Marcus Tullius Cicero, who was a Roman poet and statesman, wrote several scathing essays stating his distaste of Antony. Cicero once said:

"Now listen, I beg you, Senators, I do not mean to the personal and domestic scandals created by Antony's disgusting improprieties, but to the evil, godless way in which he has undermined us all, and our fortunes, and our whole country."

The desire to avenge the death of Caesar brought the three together. With a long list of enemies, they turned to Sextus Pompey, Cassius, and Brutus. Antony battled Cassius and Brutus at Philippi. Cassius had Brutus decapitate him so that he would not be captured. Brutus was able to escape but ended up committing suicide.

Even though Octavian was only 19 years old, he garnered the support of the majority of the Roman army, especially from those who had been loyal followers of Caesar. Octavian, in 43 BCE, demanded that the Senate provide him with political authority, which he needed. This meant a consulship. The Senate, however, refused to grant his demand since he was not even close to the age requirement of 33 years. His soldiers marched into the Senate with their swords drawn. The Senate quickly reversed its decision and provided him with a consulship as well as a co-consul, Quintus Pedius. They enacted Lex Pedia, which undid the prior ruling that had given all the conspirators immunity. The decree created a new law that condemned all of the people involved in the murder of Caesar. This included Sextus Pompey who was not even part of the actual murder.

Despite their victories, the days of the triumvirate were numbered. While Lepidus had helped with Pompey, his continued failures in battle led to Octavian banishing him to Circei. The empire was then divided between Antony and Octavian. Antony would meet Cleopatra VII of Egypt. Their love would eventually lead to war.

Antony and Cleopatra planned to trap Octavian at his fleet in Actium. Their plan was flawed from the beginning, and most of the members of Antony's team did not favor a woman having political say. Even though they outnumbered Octavian's troops, they failed. The lovers narrowly escaped; Cleopatra to Egypt and Antony to Libya. When their plans to raise more troops proved unsuccessful, the only option for Antony was suicide. Cleopatra tried her best to reach a compromise with Octavian. When this strategy failed, Cleopatra took her own life as well.

When Octavian returned to Rome, the Roman Republic was finished. Thus began the Roman Empire. He was quickly named the first emperor of Rome, Augustus. Augustus set the stage for everybody who would follow him.

Chapter 2: The Era of Empire

After the Battle of Actium, Gaius Octavian Thurinus, the heir of Caesar, was crowned the first Roman emperor. When he took over the throne, he was named Augustus Caesar. The Senate willingly gave Augustus the title of emperor. They lavished him with power and praise because he destroyed their enemies and brought stability.

Augustus ruled as emperor of Rome from 31 BCE until his death in 14 CE. During this time, he declared that he "found Rome a city of clay but left it a city of marble." Augustus was able to reform laws and secured Rome's borders. He also initiated a large number of building projects, which was mostly performed by his right-hand man, Agrippa. The first Pantheon was among these. Through all of his work, he ended up securing the name of the greatest cultural and political powers in history. He initiated what they called the Pax Romana. This was a time of prosperity and peace, which was unknown until that time and lasted over 200 years.

After Augustus died, power was passed on to Tiberius. He continued the former emperor's policies, but he lacked the vision and strength of character that defined his predecessor. This same issue continued with the three succeeding emperors:

Caligula, Claudius, and Nero. These five emperors of the Roman Empire came to be known as the Julio-Claudian Dynasty.

Caligula is commonly known for his insanity and depravity; though early on in his rule, he was actually quite commendable. This is also true for Claudius, his successor. Claudius was able to grow Rome's territory and power in Britain. Caligula and Claudius were assassinated while in office. The Praetorian Guard of Caligula murdered him, but for Claudius, it was his wife who committed the deed. Nero's suicide brought an end to the Julio-Claudian Dynasty. This caused a period of unrest among the Romans and became known as The Year of Four Emperors.

The Year of Four Emperors

The emperors that made up this period were Galba, Otho, Vitellius, and Vespasian. In 68 CE, after Nero committed suicide, Galba took over the role of emperor. He instantly proved that he was unfit for the responsibility. He, too, ended up being assassinated by the Praetorian Guard. Otho succeeded him on the very day he died. Initially, it was believed that he would make a good emperor. Unfortunately, the Romans were not able to find out. General Vitellius wanted to be in power; thus, he created a small civil war that ended in Otho committing suicide. This gave Vitellius the chance to take the throne.

He proved that he was just as unfit as Galba had been. He started engaging in luxurious feasts and entertainment instead of doing what an emperor was supposed to do. Vespasian's legions then declared that he should become emperor. Vespasian's men murdered Vitellius, and he took the throne exactly a year after Galba had ascended it.

During his rule, Vespasian created the Flavian Dynasty which was made up of empire expansion, economic prosperity, and massive building projects. Vespasian remained emperor from 69 to 79 CE. He started the construction of the Flavian Amphitheatre, which is now known as the Colosseum of Rome. Titus, his son, took over after his father's death and completed the building of the Colosseum. He ruled from 79 to 81 CE. During Titus' reign, Rome saw the eruption of Mount Vesuvius in 79 CE. The catastrophe buried the cities of Herculaneum and Pompeii.

Titus died in 81 CE from a fever. His brother, Domitian, then took over and ruled from 81 to 96 CE. He secured and expanded the Roman boundaries, and repaired the damage that had been caused by the fire. He continued the building projects began by his brother and he was also able to improve the empire's economy. Even though all of this, his autocratic policies and methods caused the Senate to dislike him. In 96 CE, Domitian was assassinated.

Five Good Emperors

Nerva took over after Domitian's assassination. Nerva created the Nervan-Antonine Dynasty, which ruled Rome from 96 to 192 CE. This period was marked by prosperity due to the five good emperors, bringing the Roman Empire to greater heights:

1. Nerva – 96 to 98 CE

2. Trajan – 98 to 117 CE

3. Hadrian – 117 to 138 CE

4. Antoninus Pius – 138 to 161 CE

5. Marcus Aurelius – 161 to 180 CE

The Roman Empire became stronger, more stable, and expanded further under their rule. Commodus and Lucius Verus were the last rulers of the Nervan-Antonine Dynasty. Verus was co-emperor under the rule of Marcus Aurelius until he died in 169 CE. It seems as though he was ineffective.

The successor and son of Aurelius, Commodus, was the biggest disgrace of all the emperors of Rome. He has depicted the world over as one who indulged his whims at the expense of Rome. He ended up being strangled in his bath by his own wrestling partner, in 192 CE. This ended the Dynasty and brought Pertinax to power.

The Severan Dynasty

For three months, Pertinax was Rome's ruler before he was assassinated. The Year of the Five Emperors then began and concluded in Septimus Severus' rise to power. He was the ruler of Rome from 193 to 211 CE. During his reign, he was able to defeat the Parthians and enlarged the size of the empire. All of his campaigns in Britain and Africa were costly and extensive. This was likely the cause of Rome's financial struggles. His successors were his sons Geta and Caracalla. Caracalla eventually had his brother killed and stayed as ruler until 217 CE, when his bodyguard killed him.

During his reign, Roman citizenship was extended to all free men in the empire. It is believed that the law was created to raise tax revenues. The Severan Dynasty continued until Alexander Severus was assassinated in 235 CE. This caused the Roman Empire to plunge into what is known as The Crisis of the Third Century

Two Empires

The time labeled as The Imperial Crisis in Roman history was marked by a never-ending civil war, as different leaders tried to gain control over the Roman Empire. There was widespread economic instability, social unrest, and the breaking up of the empire into three regions. It was Aurelian who reunited it. His policies were improved and developed upon by Diocletian who created the Tetrarchy in order to keep the empire in order.

To make the administration of such a vast empire more efficient, Diocletian halved it in 285 CE. This act created the Western and the Eastern Empires. The Eastern section is commonly referred to as the Byzantine Empire. Since the past crisis arose due to problems with succession, Diocletian declared that all future successors needed to be picked and approved at the beginning of one's rule. His two identified successors were Constantine and Maxentius. However, he did away with the rule in 305 CE, causing the tetrarchy to dissolve as the empire's regions fought for dominance. After Diocletian died in 311 CE, Constantine and Maxentius led the empire into another civil war.

Chapter 3: The Christianization, Splitting, and Fall of the Empire

Constantine was able to defeat Maxentius in 312 CE at the Battle of the Milvian Bridge. He took over as the emperor of both regions and ruled from 306 to 337 CE. Constantine strongly believed Jesus had been the reason why he won. Because of this belief, Constantine started a series of laws that specified a tolerance for the religion that became known as Christianity.

Like many other Roman emperors who believed they had a connection with some deity that improved their standing and authority, Constantine's chosen figure was Jesus Christ. In 325 CE, he presided over the First Council of Nicea to create rules for the faith. They worked to name the divinity of Jesus and how they should create the manuscript that is now known as *The Bible*. He was able to stabilize the empire, reform the military, and revalue the currency. He also managed to found the city named New Rome. It was where the former city of Byzantium stood, which eventually became known as Constantinople. It is now modern-day Istanbul.

Many Christians who saw him as a champion of their faith named him Constantine the Great. But for several historians, the honor could have also been due to his political, religious, and cultural reforms, as well as his battle skills. After he died, his sons took over the empire. They soon got involved in various conflicts, which would threaten everything that Constantine had accomplished.

Constantine's three sons, named Constans, Constantius II, and Constantine II, split the empire into thirds; but they were soon fighting over who should have more. During these conflicts, Constans and Constantine II were killed. The third brother died after he named his cousin, Julian, as his heir. Julian took over as ruler for only two years. He tried to return Rome to what it used to be through different reforms that were supposed to improve the government's efficiency.

Since Julian was a Neo-Platonic philosopher, he rejected Christian views and blamed Constantine's beliefs for the empire's decline. While he claimed to have religious tolerance, Julian got rid of all Christians in government positions, barred Christians from serving in the military, and banned the teaching of their religion. He died during his campaign against the Persians, officially ending Constantine's dynasty. He was the last pagan emperor to rule Rome. Because of his opposition to Christianity, he became known as "Julian the Apostate."

Jovian briefly ruled Rome and brought Christianity back as the main faith. He abolished several edicts Julian had established. After his death, Theodosius I became emperor. He carried on

Jovian's and Constantine's religious reforms, outlawing pagan worship in the empire, converting pagan temples to Christian churches, and closing universities and schools.

Notably, he closed Plato's Academy. A lot of his reforms were unpopular among the common people and the Roman aristocracy who still held traditional pagan practices. The unified religious beliefs and social duties were impeded by a religion that got rid of other deities, proclaiming instead that there was a single God that ruled from the heavens. Since Theodosius I was such a devout Christian, he neglected all his other duties as emperor. He ended up being the last emperor to rule the Western and Eastern Empires.

The Fall of the Empire

During 376 to 382 CE, Rome was caught up in several battles against the Goths. These became known as the Gothic Wars. On August 9, 378 CE, at the Battle of Adrianople, the Roman Emperor Valens was defeated. This is marked by historians as a pivotal point in the fall of the West.

Orosius argued that Christianity did not play a role in the fall of Rome. He believed that pagan practices were to blame instead. Some of the other influences that people believe contributed to the fall of the empire include government corruption, the large size of land, and the increasing strength of Germanic tribes. The Roman military was no longer able to keep the borders safe as they once had, nor was the government able to collect the taxes. The arrival of the Visigoths in the third century, along with the ensuing instances of rebellion, were all contributing factors to the decline of Rome.

On September 4, 476 CE, the Western Roman Empire officially ended when Romulus Augustus was killed by the German king, Odoacer. The Eastern Empire survived a while longer under the Byzantine Empire, lasting until 1453 CE. What remained no longer resembled the original empire. The Western Empire was re-invented as The Holy Roman Empire, but was a far cry from the original Roman Empire. The only similarity was in the name.

Legacy

The innovations and inventions created by the empire altered the lives of the citizens, and are still being used in many cultures around the world. Advancements in construction such as fast-drying cement, aqueducts, indoor plumbing, buildings, and roads were either created or improved by the Romans. The Western calendar came from the one that Caesar had created, and all the names of the months and days of the week are Roman in origin

Socks, newspapers, keys, locks, public toilets, and apartment complexes were created by Rome's inhabitants; as well as satire literature, magnifying glasses, cosmetics, the postal system, and shoes. During the empire's height, there were large developmental advances in warfare, government, religion, law, and medicine. Romans were adept in borrowing things and improving on them. This makes it hard to figure out what was really theirs and what was not. What we do know for sure is that they did leave an enduring legacy which still influences people today.

Chapter 4: Plebeians and Patricians

In ancient Rome, the citizens were divided between two classes: the Patricians and the Plebeians. The wealthy members of the upper class were the Patricians. The rest were referred to as Plebeians.

Patricians

The Patricians were the ruling class of the Roman Empire. There were only certain families that could be part of this class. All Patricians had to be born into the title. Though they made up a small portion of the total population of Rome, they held all the power.

Patricians were the true descendants of the original natives of Rome. Still, the origin of the class remains obscure. The issue as to when the exclusive caste was decided upon and clearly defined remains uncertain. It is believed, though, that this was through the efforts of King Servius Tullius, when he required people to register. The registration and division of citizens according to tribes and wealth created distinction between the two classes.

With the development of the Assembly of the Centuries from a military to a political group, a way was provided for wealthier Plebeians to have an influential vote in legislation and elections. The expulsion of the kings, who might have been able to check patrician control, gave the ruling class an opportunity to retain possession of religious and legal knowledge, priesthoods, and magistracies to themselves

The struggle of the Roman Republic stemmed from the continued efforts of the Plebeians to achieve political equality, to break up the religious and political monopoly set in place by the Patricians, and to secure economic relief for the poorer people.

Even though they did have a lot more power than the Plebeians, Patricians had to be careful. The Plebeians made up the majority of the population, so they could turn dangerous if angered. In order to avoid conflict, they were always faced with giving the Plebeians with just enough rights to appease them. They did their best to retain most of the power.

Towards the end of the Roman Republic, Patricians kept exclusive control only to a few positions in the priesthood, Senate leaders, and the interim head of state. During the late republic, the differences between the two classes started to lose their political importance.

Once Rome reached the empire period, having a patrician rank was a requirement for someone to ascend the throne. Only the emperor was able to create new Patricians. In order for the ancient priesthood to continue, Patricians did not have many privileges other than fewer military obligations. After the reign of Constantine ended, *Patricius* became a more personal title instead of a hereditary one of honor. It ranked third after the emperor and consuls but did not provide any sort of power.

Their responsibilities included:

- Care for and the supervision of the land.

- If they were part of the Senate, they had the responsibilities of the Senate.

Their rights included:

- Creating laws that would go to the assembly.

- Being the only people who were allowed to become senators.

- Having economic and political advantages.

Plebeians

Anybody that was not a patrician was known as a plebeian. Plebeians consisted of soldiers, laborers, craftsmen, and farmers.

Plebeians were sometimes referred to as Plebian. The distinction between the two classes was probably based on the influence and wealth of certain families who started the patrician clan under the very early republic during the fifth and fourth centuries BCE.

Originally, Plebeians were not allowed to join the Senate or any other public office except for the military tribune. Before the 445 BCE passage of the Lex Canuleia law, they could only marry other Plebeians.

Their responsibilities included:

- Fighting in the Roman army.

- Working for the Patricians' land.

Unfortunately, Plebeians did not have any rights because they were merely seen as "common folk." Eventually, though, they fought and were given the right to participate in politics.

Early Rome

There were a lot of differences between the Plebeians and Patricians. These included responsibilities and rights, power levels, and population levels, among other things. Patricians wanted to make sure that they retained the majority of the power, but they needed to have the Plebeians on their side to do it.

The Plebeians had very little rights during the early stages of Rome. Every single religious and government position was held by a patrician. They were the ones who created the laws, owned all of the lands, and held the position of general in the army.

Plebeians were not allowed to hold any sort of public office and they could not even marry Patricians.

Since the Plebeians worked as foot soldiers, they fought most of the Roman battles and helped in Rome's expansion. This meant that they expanded the influence that the Patricians had. Patricians were often resented for the power they held, but the Patricians likely feared the Plebeians because they made up a large portion of the population.

Since being plebeian or patrician was based on family relations, no intermarriage was allowed during the early days of Rome. In order to make sure that the Plebeians continued to fight their wars, they later changed this law.

Plebeian Revolt

At around 494 BCE, the Plebeians started to fight against the rules established by the Patricians. This was known as the "Conflict of the Orders." During the course of around 200 years, the Plebeians made attempts to obtain more rights. They went on strike in order to protest. They left the city for a long while, refusing to work or fight in the army. Eventually, through several revolts, the Plebeians they were able to gain a number of rights, which included being allowed to run for office and to marry Patricians.

Their campaign lasted until 287 BCE. The Plebeians organized themselves into different corporations and withdrew from the state during at least five critical occasions in order to compel the Patricians to concede. One such time was when their withdrawal was called secession.

The plebeian group held their own assemblies and elected their own officials. These tribunes were normally Plebeians who were more well-to-do than the others. The most important step in the campaign of the Plebeians was achieving the inviolability of their tribunes. The campaign ended when Quintus Hortensius, a plebeian dictator, was appointed. He created the law, Lex Hortensia, which made approved measures in their assembly binding; not only to the Plebeians but to the entire community. Later in the Republic and in the Empire as well, the term was still used to describe any of the commoners.

The Law of Twelve Tables

One of the first concessions that the Plebeians saw after their revolt was the Law of the Twelve Tables. These laws were displayed in public where everybody could see them. They were put in place to protect most of the basic rights of Roman citizens, no matter what their social class was.

The Twelve Tables were supposed to have been written by ten commissioners, at the insistence of the Plebeians. They felt that their legal rights had been hampered by the fact that the judgments were based on unwritten customs preserved by a very small group of Patricians.

They started in 451, and the first set of commissioners created ten tables. These were then supplemented with two additional tables later on. All were formally posted in 450. They were likely written on bronze tablets and placed in the Roman Forum. This written code allowed the Plebeians to become more acquainted with the law, helping to protect them against any abuse of power on the Patricians' part.

These Twelve Tables were not a liberalizing of a certain custom or a reform. Instead, they recognized the feelings of the patrician class and the patriarchal family, the interference of religion in civil cases, and the validity of enslavement for debts that had not been paid.

The fact that they show a remarkable amount of liberality for their time when it comes to testamentary rights and contract, has probably less to do with the innovations of decemvirs, and more to do with the progress that had been made in commercial customs during a time of vigorous trade and prosperity.

Since there are only a few random quotations from the Twelve Tables that are extant today, knowledge about what they actually contained largely comes from the reference in later juridical writings. While they were held in high honor by Romans as the prime legal source, they were superseded through later changes in the law but were never actually abolished.

The following are what we know about what the twelve tables covered:

- Table 1 – procedure for trials and courts.

- Table 2 – continuation for trails and theft.

- Table 3 – how debt is handled.

- Table 4 – the rights of the fathers over their family.

- Table 5 – the legal inheritance and guardianship laws.

- Table 6 – acquisition and possession.

- Table 7 – land rights and crimes.

- Table 8 – torts and delicts.

- Table 9 – the public law.

- Table 10 – the sacred law.

- Table 11 – supplemental information one.

- Table 12 – supplemental information two.

Plebeian Officers

Eventually, Plebeians got to elect their own officials in the government. These people were known as tribunes who represented the other Plebeians and who fought for their kind's rights. They were able to veto new laws that the Roman Senate created.

Plebeian Nobles

As time passed, there were fewer legal differences between the Patricians and Plebeians. The Plebeians were able to be elected to the Senate and they were even allowed to hold the title of consul. Furthermore, Plebeians were allowed to get married to Patricians. Wealthy Plebeians even ended up becoming part of the Roman nobility. However, even though there were a lot of changes in their laws, the Patricians always had most of the power and wealth in Ancient Rome.

Chapter 5: A Melting Pot of Theism

In most societies, whether they are modern or ancient, religion has played a major role during their development. In the beginning, the religion of Rome was polytheistic. Rome had an array of spirits and gods, and more were added to include foreign cults and Greek gods. When the empire began to expand, Romans did not impose their beliefs on the people they conquered. This should not be thought of as tolerance, as proven in the way that they responded to the Christian and Jewish population. Christianity would eventually replace all of these gods.

Early Influences and Beliefs

The earliest form of religion in Rome was animistic. They believed spirits inhabited everything, including people. The citizens thought they were watched by their ancestors' spirits. In the beginning, a Capitoline Triad was added to the spirits. These new gods were Mars, Quirinus, and Jupiter. Mars was the god of war and thought to be the father of Remus and Romulus, the founders of Rome. Quirinus was Romulus after he had been deified. He watched over all the inhabitants of Rome. Jupiter was a supreme god. These three, as well as several others, were worshipped at Capitoline Hill. Because of the Etruscans, this triad will change and include Jupiter as the supreme god; Minerva, who was Jupiter's daughter; and Juno, who was his sister and wife.

Through the influence of Greek colonies found across the Lower Peninsula, many of the gods worshiped in Greece were taken in by the Romans. Myth and religion were one. Roman gods were more anthropomorphic because of the Greek influence. They now had human characteristics of hate, love, jealousy, etc. Romans believed that individual expression was not important, but strict adherence to rituals was. By doing this, they avoided the problems of religious zeal. Each city would come up with its own set of deities and would perform its own religious rites. They built temples throughout the empire to honor their gods. These temples were the god's home and worship was done outside of the temple. Even though the fusion of Greek and Roman deities did influence Rome in a lot of ways, their religion stayed very practical.

They had four separate colleges for priests, although they did not have a priestly class. It was a public office, not a holy one. This practice extended all the way to the imperial palace. Emperor Augustus took the title of chief priest. Besides the chief priest, some individuals had the ability to read a bird's flight. Others could read the entrails of animals in order to find out the will of the gods, or interpret omens. They would perform elaborate rituals in order to bring victory to Rome during battle. They never went into war or declared war without approval from the gods. From Etruscans times, a diviner was always consulted. They believed that it was very bad to ignore omens. A Roman soothsayer, Spurinna, saw Julius Ceasar's death on the Ides of March upon reading animal entrails. One Roman Commander, Publius Claudius Pulcher, ignored omens and did not eat the sacred chicken before battle during the First Punic War. He was defeated and his military career ended.

The Pantheon

When studying Roman mythology, the emphasis is put on major gods like Juno, Pluto, Neptune, and Jupiter. There were also many minor goddesses and gods like Pax, Cupid, Nemesis, and the Furies.

When you look at Roman religion, you have to look at the impact from the important gods. Foremost are Jupiter and his sister/wife Juno. Jupiter was the sky god, the king of the gods. He controlled the weather and the forces of nature, using thunderbolts to warn the Romans. He was originally the farming god but his role began changing as the city's size got larger. He eventually had his own temple at Capitoline Hill. His supremacy was temporarily set aside while during the reign of Emperor Elagabalus, who replaced Rome's top deity with the Syrian god, Elagabal. Once the emperor was assassinated, Alexander Severus returned Jupiter to his rightful place. Juno came next. She was Jupiter's sister/wife. The month June is named after her. She is a supreme goddess who has her own temple on Esquiline Hill. She is believed to be the goddess of the moon and light. She shows all of the virtues of matronhood. As the goddess of fertility and childbirth, she is Juno Lucina.

Next, come Minerva, and Mars, the war god. Legend states that Minerva sprang out of Jupiter's head. A goddess of education, industry, and commerce, she would later on be regarded as the goddess of war, craftsmen, musicians, and doctors. Mars has a temple that was dedicated by Emperor Augustus to honor the death of the assassins of Julius Caesar. Sacrifices would be made to him before and after battles by Roman commanders. The day of the week, Tuesday, was named after him.

Cult Worship

Other than worshipping the above gods, the Romans worshiped many cults such as the Imperial Cult, Sibyl, Sarapis, Isis, Cybele, and Bacchus. Some of these were accepted by society while others brought fear. Bacchus was a wine god. He is the main reason for the festivals that took place on March 17th. On this day, a young Roman would become a man. As this continued, the Senate soon realized how dangerous this could be, and abolished it in 186 BCE. This only sent the group underground.

Cybele was worshipped by another cult. She was a fertility goddess who has her own temple on Palatine Hill. She is responsible for the well-being of the people. She arrived in Athens in the 5th century BCE, and showed up in Rome in the middle of the Punic Wars. The eunuchs were her priests. Majority of her followers castrated themselves.

Isis is an ancient goddess from Egypt. You might remember her from Egyptian mythology as the mother of Horus and wife of Osiris. Once she became Hellenized, she was the protector of fishermen and sailors.

Sarapis came to Rome from Alexandria. She is the healing god. Sick people would travel miles to be cured at her temple. Sibyl was a priestess of Apollo and traveled from the colony of Cumae in Greece, to Rome. She offered the nine Sibylline Books to the Etruscan King Tarquin. These books are full of prophecies but the king refused because her price was too high. After six of the books were burned, the King reconsidered and decided to buy the remaining three. The Senate consulted these books during emergencies. Unfortunately, they were lost during the barbarian invasion in the fifth century CE.

The thought of deifying an emperor came to life during Emperor Augustus' reign. He would not let the Senate name him a god because he thought he was the son of a god. When he died, the Senate gave him the deification. This was bestowed on many of his successors but some were not bestowed with such distinction. These were Domitian, Nero, Caligula, and Tiberius. They were considered too disgusting to be given such an honor. Nero and Caligula thought they were living gods, and Domitian thought he was the reincarnated Hercules.

Religion Challenged

Christianity and Judaism both posed threats to Rome. They had something in common, as these beliefs refused to worship the Roman gods or make sacrifices to them. Even though the Jews had a firm establishment in the Empire, they were always the target of emperors and were often blamed for everything bad that happened within the empire. Nero even went so far as to banish them out of Rome. Titus continued the war against them during the Jewish Wars. They eventually destroyed Jerusalem and killed thousands.

Christianity was first considered as a sect of Judaism. Nero became suspicious when the Christian group began growing in number. The Great Fire was blamed on the Christians. In retaliation, they called Nero the anti-Christ. In time, Christianity would spread throughout Rome. It appealed to the slaves, women, the illiterate, and the intellectuals. Persecutions got worse and Christian churches were burned. All these continued while Diocletian reigned, ending with the Great Persecution. The Romans thought that Christians offended the "peace of the gods."

Under the reign of Constantine, Christianity received recognition from the Edict of Milan during 313 CE. His compassion toward Christians goes back to the Battle of Milvan Bridge. He believed he saw a cross form in the sky. He thought this vision caused him to be victorious in battle and to become the emperor of Rome. He held a Council of Nicaea in 325 CE, reconciling the differences between the many Christian sects. Under him, churches that had been destroyed were rebuilt. Some people say that he became a Christian on his deathbed. Christianity would eventually grow and replace all of the traditional religions of Rome. This would make Rome the new Christian center. Yet, Christianity would still take the blame for the misfortunes that happened in the empire. Many people blame the fall of the empire on Christianity. Edward Gibbon thought Christianity absorbed the people's energy and made them unable to handle the problems that were plaguing the empire. In spite of all its lows and highs, beginning from the days of inhabiting spirits to all the gods and goddesses, emperor deification, and on to Christianity, religion has always been an important part of the Roman Empire.

Chapter 6: The Masterpiece That Was Rome

Roman art suffered a crisis to their reputation since it was discovered that the majority actually came from ancient Greece during the 1600s CE and onwards. Once art critics realized that most of the finest pieces were merely copies of some lost Greek originals, they did not appreciate it as much. Roman art had flourished with everything Roman during the Renaissance and medieval times but soon diminished. There were other problems with Roman art such as not really identifying what it actually was. It differed from Greek art, and geography played a big role. It was more diverse as it changed according to location. Even though Rome remained the main focal point, there were other centers that produced art in accordance with the respective tastes and trends of a locality. The most notable are Athens, Antioch, and Alexandria. Because of this, many critics argue that Roman art does not actually exist.

Nowadays, there is a more balanced view of Roman art. Successes in archaeology have caused Roman art to be reviewed, and its contribution to the western world has been made clearer. People hold the opinion that Classical Greek art was the pinnacle of artistic endeavors. Many think that Romans simply fused Etruscan and the best of Greek art. They admit that Roman art is very eclectic, inheriting traits from the Hellenistic world that was forged by Alexander the Great and all his conquests. Since this empire covers a very large and diverse culture, the way in which people appreciated the past and depicted vivid ideas to commemorate persons and events are expressed in various art forms. Coins, epigraphy, monumental architecture, statues, frescoes, pottery, mosaics, glassware, jewelry, and seal-cutting were all created to make Rome more beautiful. It also conveyed various meanings in fashion and the military.

Works of art were taken from conquered cities and brought to Rome for the citizens to appreciate them. Artists from other countries were employed by the Romans, and they opened schools. They established technical development centers and workshops all over the place. The demand for artwork increased, giving rise to mass production. Objects soon flooded the entire empire. The number of artwork that has survived over the years is mind-blowing. Consider Pompeii. It shows a rare insight into the way that works of art were used to enrich the citizens' lives. It became more personalized and individuals owned many pieces. This can be seen in the creation of lifelike portraits of private citizens, through sculptures and paintings. Unlike other civilizations, art was accessible to the lower classes, not just the wealthy.

Roman Sculpture

These sculptures were blended from the idealized perfection of Classical Greek sculptures, with a greater enthusiasm for realism mixed in. Romans sculptors have preserved invaluable works of art that may have been lost.

By the middle of the first century CE, artists in Rome were trying to create and capture the optical effects of shade and light to create more realism. This type of art was developed from keeping wax funeral masks of dead family members. These were then transferred into stone, producing private busts that would show the subject as flabby, scarred, wrinkled, or old. These busts tell the truth. During the antiquity period, there was a strong move toward impressionism that used abstract forms and tricks of light. Sculptures also became massive and monumental, with larger-than-life statues of heroes, gods, and emperors. This style is much like the bronze statue of Marcus Aurelius sitting on top of the horse that is in the Capitoline Museum, Rome. Towards the end of the Empire, sculptures began to lack proportion. The heads were often large and figures were flatter, often displaying an influence from Eastern art.

The sculpture on altars and buildings could either be for political purposes or just decorative. Some arches captured in great detail special events showing a certain emperor being victorious. It gave the world a message that this emperor was not to be messed with.

Roman Wall Paintings

The insides of the Roman building were decorated with bold designs. Stucco was utilized to create relief effects. In the first century BCE, military structures, tombs, temples, private homes, and public buildings all across made use of fresco and wall paintings. Designs ranged from impressionistic renderings to realistic details that would cover the ceiling and every available inch of space.

Painters used natural earth tones like dark browns, yellows, and reds. Black and blue were employed for plainer designs. The usual subjects depicted in paintings include architecture, mythological scenes, portraits, fauna, flora, entire gardens, landscapes, and townscapes creating 360-degree panoramas that transport the viewer from a small room to the wide world of the artist's imagination.

Roman Mosaics

These pieces were common in many homes and public places across the empire, from Antioch to Africa. Mosaics were created with small colored squares of shells, stone, pottery, glass, tile, or marble. Each piece measured around .5 and 1.5 cm. but contained fine details. Designs would have a large spectrum of colors and used colored grout to match.

The most popular subjects were scenes of fauna, flora, food, hunting, agriculture, sports, gladiator contests, and mythology. They would even create realistic portraits of Romans. The most famous is from the House of the Faun, Pompeii, showing Alexander the Great on the back of Bucephalus doing battle with Darius III, who is in his war chariot.

Architectural Orders

Architects followed the guidelines that were established by the Classical Greeks like Corinthian, Ionic, and Doric. The Romans, though, favored the Corinthian style in their buildings. They did add their own versions and ideas to the Corinthian capital and became more decorative. There is also a mixture of the volute of the Ionic order and the acanthus leaves of the Corinthian. The Tuscan column was also adapted, which was formed from a Doric column but had a smaller capital, a molded base, and a slender shaft without flutes. This column was used in domestic homes like verandahs and peristyles. Monolithic columns were favored instead of the stacking of many drums on top of each other.

As the Empire continued to expand, craftsmen and ideas became integrated into the architectural industry, many using familiar materials such as marble. The eastern influence is seen in features like ornamental fountains, street colonnades, sculptured pedestals, and papyrus leaves in capitals.

Techniques and Materials

The Temple of Jupiter Stator in Rome was the first building to be made entirely of marble. Marble was not widely used until the Empire period. The marble that came from foreign countries were reserved mainly for columns and imperial projects.

Travertine white limestone was preferred for carvings and could hold up heavy loads. It was a favorite substitute for marble and was mainly utilized for steps, window and door frames, as well as paving.

Architects

Buildings were credited to the persons who conceived the projects and paid for them instead of the architects overseeing their construction. Because of this, architects often remained anonymous. Usually, only architects who were employed by the emperor were well-known. Trajan had a favored architect, Apollodorus of Damascus. His skills were building bridges but he is also recognized for building the Trajan's Forum and Baths in Rome. Celer and Severus were responsible for the magnificent sounding roof on Nero's Golden House.

The most famous architect is Vitruvius. He constructed a basilica in Fano and worked for Augustus and Julius Ceasar. He wrote *On Architecture,* a ten-volume study about the subject. The set of books has survived, completely intact, all these years. It covers all facets of architecture, including advice for people who want to be architects, types of buildings, and a lot more. A quote from Vitruvius sums it up: "All buildings must be executed in such a way as to take account of durability, utility, and beauty."

Key Buildings

Bridges and Aqueducts:

These were massive structures that could have single, double, or triple tiers of arches. They were designed to carry fresh water from sources many miles away.

Basilicas:

These buildings were adopted by the Christian church but were originally built as places for large gatherings, commonly being courts of law. The structure was usually constructed beside the city's marketplace. It was enclosed by colonnades on every side. The basilica's roof and the long hall were likewise supported by piers and columns. The columns form a central nave flanked on every side by an aisle. A gallery runs all around the first floor and an altar is found at either one or both ends. A good example is the Severan Basilica that is located at Lepcis Magna.

Baths:

Roman baths show how well the Romans were at creating breathtaking interior spaces using buttresses, vaults, domes, and arches. The largest was built symmetrically on a single axis and included underfloor heating, libraries, fountains, hot and cold rooms, pools, and inner-wall heating with terracotta piping. The exteriors were normally plain, but the interiors were full of mosaics, statues, marble, and columns. The best surviving example is the Baths of Caracalla located in Rome.

Private Homes:

All of these are famous for their sumptuously decorated interiors through the use of stucco and fresco. These residences might also have fountains, gardens, peristyles, and atriums, all fitting harmoniously together. A good example is the House of the Vettii at Pompeii.

Temples:

Roman temples were a combination of the Greek and Etruscan models. They had an inner chamber at the back of the building that was surrounded by columns and was built on a platform that had a stepped entrance with a columned porch. The columned porch was the focal point of the building. The Maison Carree at Nimes is a complete example. Most temples were rectangular but could also take the shape of a polygon or a circle. The temple of Venus at Baalbeck is a polygonal one.

Amphitheater and Theaters:

Roman theatres are, of course, inspired by the Greeks. The main difference was the orchestra pit that was built in a semi-circular shape, with the entire theatre made from stone. Romans added in a decorated stage building that had many different statues, pediments, projections, and levels of columns. The theatre at Orange is a good example.

The completely enclosed amphitheater was a Roman's favorite. The Colosseum is the most famous and also the largest. It has a highly decorative exterior and the seats are set over many barrel vaults. Underground rooms are situated below the floor of the arena, hiding props, animals and people until they were needed.

Triumphal Arches:

These had triple, double, or a single entrance. They had no practical function but were built to commemorate significant events like military victories.

Walls:

Roman walls have many variations. The width of these walls ranges from a thin 18 centimeters to a massive six meters. They never used stone blocks or marble. Masonry walls were created out of square blocks and built without the application of mortar. They commonly utilized brick and small stones that faced a concrete core.

Conclusion

Thank you for making it through to the end of *Ancient Rome*. We hope it was informative and was able to provide you with all of the tools you needed to achieve your goals, whatever they may be.

Ancient Rome was an amazing place set amidst an interesting time. There is more to its history that we have yet to uncover. It is fun to imagine what it would have been like to live in ancient Rome. While we cannot actually be there, reading about it provides a richer experience.

With that, we have come to the end of this book. I want to thank you for choosing this book.

Now that you have come to the end of this book, we would first like to express our gratitude for choosing this particular source and taking the time to read through it. All the information here was well researched and put together in a way to help you understand the Ancient Greece as easily as possible.

We hope you found it useful and you can now use it as a guide anytime you want. You may also want to recommend it to any family or friends that you think might find it useful as well.

Finally, if you found this book useful in any way, a review is always appreciated!

CPSIA information can be obtained
at www.ICGtesting.com
Printed in the USA
LVHW091504160921
697900LV00012B/3